A Note to Parents

Dorling Kindersley Readers is a compelling program for beginning readers, designed in conjunction with leading literacy experts.

Beautiful illustrations and superb full-color photographs combine with engaging, easy-to-read stories to offer a fresh approach to each subject in the series. Each *Dorling Kindersley Reader* is guaranteed to capture a child's interest while developing his or her reading skills, general knowledge, and love of reading.

The four levels of *Dorling Kindersley Readers* are aimed at different reading abilities, enabling you to choose the books that are exactly right for your child:

Level 1 – Beginning to read
Level 2 – Beginning to read alone
Level 3 – Reading alone
Level 4 – Proficient readers

The "normal" age at which a child begins to read can be anywhere from three to eight years old, so these levels are only a general guideline.

No matter which level you select, you can be sure that you are helping your child learn to read, then read to learn!

LONDON, NEW YORK, DELHI, PARIS,
MUNICH, and JOHANNESBURG

Project Editor David John
Designer Guy Harvey
Publishing Manager Cynthia O'Neill
Art Director Cathy Tincknell
Senior DTP Designer
Andrew O'Brien
Production Nicola Torode
US Editor Gary Werner

First American Edition, 2001

00 01 02 03 04 05 10 9 8 7 6 5 4 3 2 1

Published in the United States by
Dorling Kindersley Publishing, Inc.
95 Madison Avenue
New York, New York 10016

www.wcw.com

Published in Great Britain by Dorling Kindersley Limited.

Printed and bound in China.

A Cataloging-in-Publication record is available from the Library of Congress.

0-7894-7353-4 [pb] 0-7894-7354-2 [plc]

All photographic images provided by
World Championship Wrestling, Inc.

see our complete catalog at

www.dk.com

Contents

FINISHING MOVES

Written by Michael Teitelbaum

PROFICIENT 4 READERS

A Dorling Kindersley Book

***Nitro* Fever!**
WCW's live TV show *Nitro* first went on the air in 1995. It was an instant success. After a few months, the show was extended from one hour to two. Wrestling soon became the hugely popular sport it is today.

WCW in the house!

The lights dim in the giant arena. Fireworks explode, and loud music blares from the speakers as spotlights sweep through the crowd. The atmosphere is part circus, part rock concert, and all fun. It's time for another night of World Championship Wrestling, one of the most popular spectacles in sports.

Excitement builds in a packed stadium as fans wait for WCW's superstar wrestlers to appear.

Why is wrestling so great? The answer is—the wrestlers! They are among the fittest athletes in the world. Wrestling superstars have huge muscles, and huge personalities, too. Each has a distinct look, attitude, and most of all, flamboyant finishing move.

The finishing move is the special maneuver a wrestler uses to win the match. It is like a signature—one of a kind, and instantly recognizable.

This book shows how each wrestler develops his own finishing move. It introduces the classic wrestling techniques on which all finishing moves are based. It ends with a look at the biggest stars, and the moves they have made their own.

No break!
Wrestlers often perform nightly with almost no break. They have to spend hours in the gym, building up their muscles, so that they can execute the moves that fill each match.

Superstar The Total Package knows it's important to train hard.

Listen up! Don't try to copy wrestling moves at home. It's not safe, and it's not smart! Leave the wrestling to the pros!

First steps

Every WCW wrestler takes safety very seriously. After all, the point is to win, not to get badly injured or to injure a fellow professional.

That's why the first step toward creating a devastating finishing move is learning how to wrestle safely. Many would-be wrestlers learn these lessons at a training school called the Power Plant. This is a "wrestling academy" based in Atlanta, Georgia. Here, instructors train wrestlers before they enter the ring. Recruits learn the basic wrestling moves—and how to fight without getting hurt!

Training is not just about looking good. Goldberg keeps in shape to keep safe and injury-free.

Over time, the wrestlers gain experience, confidence, and strength. They learn the limits of their bodies and start to develop their own unique wrestling personalities.

Finally, they get creative in their moves. Only then are they ready to step into the WCW spotlights.

Graduate
WCW champion Goldberg is a graduate of the Power Plant training school.

An instructor at the Power Plant puts new recruits through their paces.

Drop and Fall
This move is really another use of the leglock. It suits agile, fast-moving wrestlers. They can drop to the mat, then use a leglock to make their opponents lose balance and fall over.

Basic moves

All finishing moves are variations on basic maneuvers. These are the classic moves that grapplers learn before they step into the ring.

The leglock is a popular basic maneuver. One of the quickest ways to get an opponent down to the mat is to attack his "wheels" (his feet and legs). Once the opponent is down, the other wrestler can pin him, or place him in a leglock submission hold, until he "gives in."

Wrestling legend Ric Flair (right) *locks legs with The Franchise.*

Booker T. holds Sting in a headlock.

The headlock is another useful basic move. If a wrestler traps an opponent in a headlock, he forces his rival to spend energy. The other wrestler gets tired, as he tries to struggle free.

Also, while the victim struggles, the wrestler applying the headlock gets a chance to catch his breath. He can plot his next move. A headlock is a great way to slow down the pace of a match, especially against a fast-moving opponent.

Old move
The headlock may be one of the oldest wrestling moves ever invented. The ancient Greeks used it in their wrestling matches thousands of years ago!

Up you go
A trainee wrestler at the Power Plant learns how to perform a body slam safely.

Wrestlers with strong arms and shoulders often carry out the basic move called the body slam. They use their strength to lift their rivals into the air, before slamming them back onto the mat.

The suplex is a more difficult move. The wrestler holds his opponent in a headlock and lifts him straight up into the air. Then both the wrestler performing the move and his victim go crashing to the mat!

Bam Bam Bigelow performs a suplex.

This dangerous move must be performed with care and precision. Many wrestlers learn the suplex early in their careers, but it takes years to master.

A member of Kronik (right) *prepares to slam his opponent to the mat.*

Think ahead
All wrestlers need to "wrestle smart" and plan their battles in advance. Many WCW stars are used to smart thinking. Disco Inferno (*above*) went to business school. Other wrestlers have studied medicine and psychology!

Good plan!
Most wrestlers focus on their own strengths. They also use moves that exploit their opponents' weaknesses.

Most WCW action takes place on the mat. However, some wrestlers prefer to launch their finishing moves by soaring through the air! They carry out these dangerous, catlike leaps from the top rope, often taking their opponents by surprise.

Mike Awesome carries out an air raid on Kanyon using a devastating "Flying Clothesline" move.

This airborne style was first introduced to WCW by the "lucha libre" wrestlers of Mexico. It is especially popular with lighter wrestlers, such as Kidman and Rey Mysterio, Jr.

These fast-moving guys weigh under 230 pounds and compete in the cruiserweight division. But don't let their size fool you. Sometimes cruiserweights can defeat wrestlers who weigh between 300 and 400 pounds!

Taking a dive
Some wrestlers practice their high-flying moves from the diving board of a swimming pool. That way if the move goes wrong, they go splash, not splat! Here, Vampiro performs his finishing move, the Nail in the Coffin.

Finding your finish

So you've mastered the basics. Your leglock can trap Big Poppa Pump. Your headlock can hold 6'11" Kevin Nash. Your suplex can stun even Goldberg, and your body slam flattens *both* of Kronik. That's great! Now, how do you develop a finishing move that is all your own?

Sarge
Sgt. Buddy Lee Parker joined the Power Plant as head trainer after 13 years as a pro wrestler. He's known as Sarge, because he's in charge!

Paul Orndorff explains how to carry out a leglock.

Most WCW wrestlers develop a finishing move during their training days at the Power Plant. They get guidance from the two trainers there—Paul Orndorff and Sgt. Buddy Lee Parker, known simply as "Sarge."

The two trainers look at each recruit's strengths. Some wrestlers are big and powerful. Others are fast and can move quickly around the ring. Orndorff and Sarge help each wrestler to develop a finishing move that builds on these strengths. They also think about each wrestler's personality, to help a move develop.

That's how a finishing move is born. The Franchise took a suplex, and turned it into the Pittsburgh Plunge. Sting took a leglock, and the Scorpion Deathlock was born!

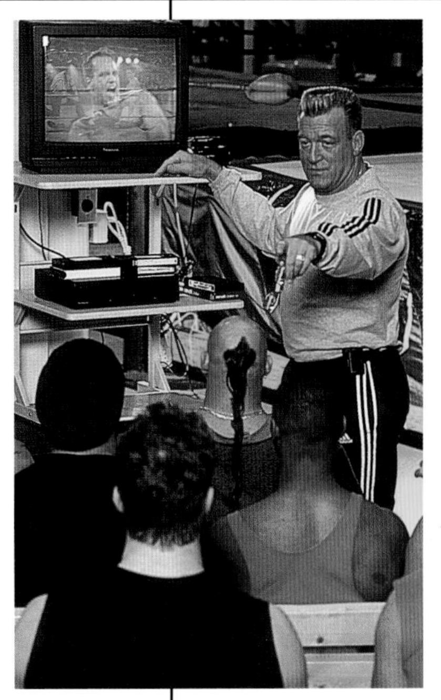

Mr. Wonderful
Paul Orndorff was a pro wrestler in the 1980s and early 1990s. He held the WCW TV title, plus three tag team championships with two different partners. In the mid-1990s, he left the ring to train future champions.

The ultimate finish
In many ways, the pin is wrestling's ultimate finishing move. In most cases, all the fancy footwork, acrobatics, and feats of strength come down to holding an opponent's shoulders on the mat for the three-count!

Rules of the match

A finishing move is all about winning a match. The rules of wrestling clearly spell out what it takes to win. They also explain what it takes to be disqualified, and lose.

There are three ways to win. The first is to pin your opponent to the mat for a count of three. If the referee counts one-two-three, slamming his hand on the mat with each count, the match is over.

Buff Bagwell pins Brian Adams to the mat for a three-count.

The referee counts down as Booker T. pins Sting to the mat.

The second way to win is to get your opponent into a powerful hold, from which he can't escape. In the end, the victim taps the mat three times. This shows the referee that the wrestler has had enough, and it is called a "tap out."

Finally, a wrestler wins a match when his opponent hits the mat and can't get up again in the time it takes the referee to count to 10. If a wrestler is down, and the ref counts slowly to 10 before he gets up, the other wrestler has won!

Two down
Sometimes, after an intense collision, both wrestlers hit the mat. As they try to get up the referee counts to 10. The first one up before the referee reaches 10 is the winner.

Bad Boy
Mike Awesome is often disqualified for illegal actions. These include breaking tables over his opponents' backs!

Wrestlers can be disqualified from a match for breaking the rules in a number of ways. For a start, it is illegal to carry objects such as chairs or baseball bats into the ring. The exception to this is a hardcore match, where anything goes.

Wrestlers are also disqualified for a "run-in." This is when a friend comes into the ring to interfere with a match. If the referee cannot get the intruder to leave, he disqualifies his buddy instead!

Mike Awesome doesn't always play by the rules!

Nine seconds
Often you will see wrestlers who have slipped out of the ring take a nine-second breather. They scoot back into the ring just before the referee counts "10."

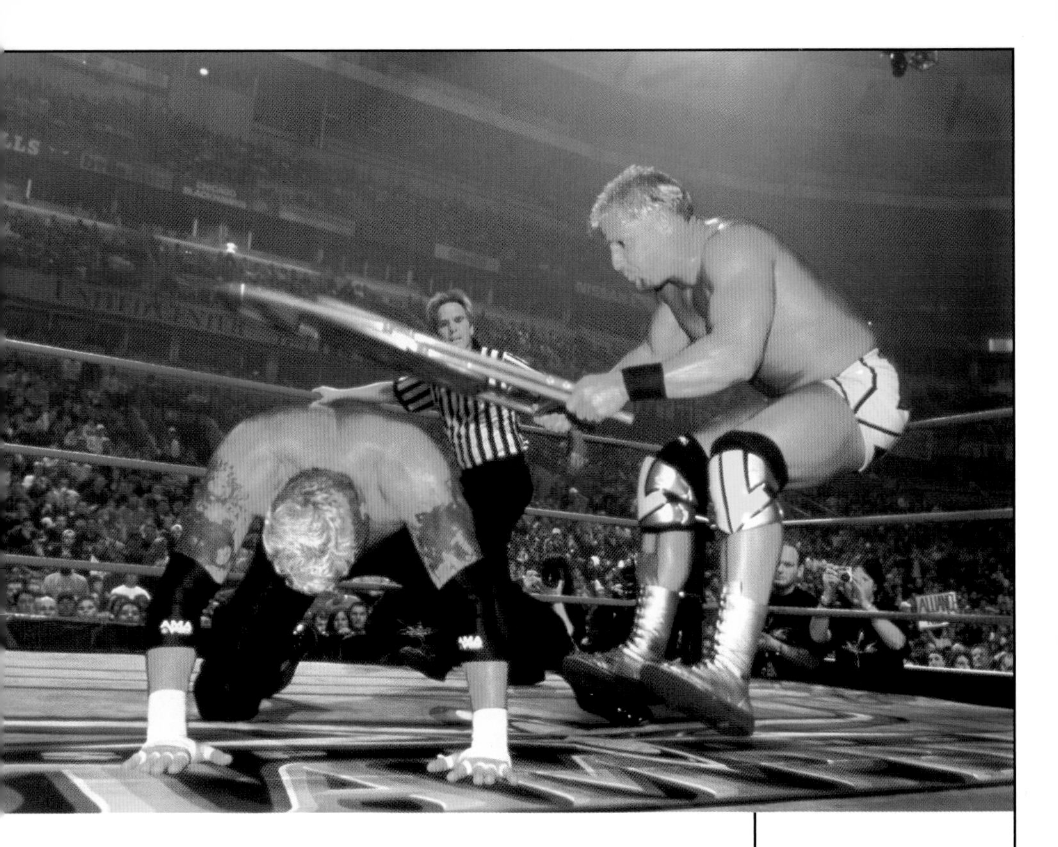

Jeff Jarrett slams Diamond Dallas Page with a metal chair—a highly illegal move!

A wrestler who leaves the ring for more than 10 seconds, for whatever reason, will be counted out by the referee and disqualified.

If the referee spots an illegal move, such as a choke hold, he will start to count to five. If the offending wrestler doesn't release the hold by the time the referee reaches five, he is disqualified.

And the very fastest way to be disqualified? Just touch the referee. Plain and simple. You are history!

No Holds Barred
Sometimes a wrestler keeps up an illegal hold for the first four seconds of the ref's five-count. He releases the hold just as the referee reaches "five."

Work it!
Goldberg needs to lift jumbo-sized opponents high over his head for the monster Jackhammer. Some of them weigh more than 300 pounds! So he trains hard to keep up his strength.

Goldberg

You've heard about the training, the basic moves, and the rules of the match. Now read about the finishing moves that some of the most famous WCW stars use to win.

Goldberg is a good place to start. His moves, the Spear and Jackhammer, helped him build a streak of 175 consecutive victories.

First, he levels his victim with the Spear, a variation on a football tackle. Then comes the Jackhammer. It usually ends the match!

*Goldberg flattens Sting with the Spear (*left*).*

*The Jackhammer (*right*).*

Rebel, rebel
Nash was a founding member of the renegade groups called the New World Order and the Wolfpac. Both battled for control of WCW.

The Commissioner
Nash was once Commissioner of WCW. He abused his authority. For example, he took the WCW world heavyweight title away from Sid Vicious and awarded it to himself, without a match!

Kevin Nash

Kevin Nash's finishing move is called the Jack Knife Powerbomb. The powerbomb is a forceful move when a normal-sized wrestler performs it, but Nash is 6'11" and 370 pounds, so his version leads to total chaos!

Nash prepares to unleash the Jack Knife Powerbomb.

Nash is almost unbeatable. He's won four WCW tag team championships and three WCW heavyweight titles.

He's also a contender for the title of "baddest bad boy" in WCW history. On one occasion, he caused chaos by powerbombing the former WCW vice president, Eric Bischoff, right through an interview stage! These days, he's known more for his bad-boy behavior than his victories in the ring.

Outsiders
Even someone of Nash's size couldn't floor Goldberg with the powerbomb. Instead, he brought an end to Goldberg's long winning streak with some help from his fellow outsider, Scott Hall (*above*).

Scott Steiner

This wrestler's finishing move is called the Steiner Recliner. It's a variation on the basic headlock. Only in this case, Scott Steiner sits on his opponent, as if on a recliner chair, and traps the victim's chin so that he can't move.

Following years of "pumpin' iron" at the gym, Steiner is amazingly strong. The power in his huge arms makes the Steiner Recliner a submission hold that almost always brings Big Poppa Pumpa victory.

Big Poppa Pump
Steiner earned the nickname "Big Poppa Pump" because of his huge, muscular arms.

Scott Steiner shows Sid Vicious who's the boss with the Steiner Recliner.

Steiner's career took off when he won six WCW tag team titles with his brother Rick. But when fellow wrestlers Kevin Nash and Scott Hall formed the outlaw New World Order, Scott joined the bad boys.

Since then, he has set out on his own, winning the WCW US title three times. For a while, he joined the New Blood, a group formed by WCW heads Vince Russo and Eric Bischoff. However, he soon went back to wrestling as an independent.

Family custom
Scott gets a taste of his own medicine from his brother Rick (*above*).

Big in Japan
Scott Steiner often battles in Japan, where he has many fans. He has won several Japanese wrestling titles, and his matches fill 50,000-seat stadiums.

Changing face Sting's look has changed a number of times *(above and below)*. He now wears black-and-white facepaint.

Sting

Sting has worked his way up the WCW ladder rung by rung. He's become one of the biggest names in wrestling along the way. One reason for his success may be the fact that he's perfected no fewer than three finishing moves. Most wrestlers only master one!

Early in his career, Sting used the Stinger Splash. First he slammed his opponent against the turnbuckle. Then he crushed him with a leaping bodypress.

Next, he won seven world heavyweight championships using the Scorpion Deathlock.

When Sting wrestled with the rebel Wolfpac group, he wore red facepaint.

It's a variation on the classic "figure-four" leglock. Sting has turned this simple hold into a crushing maneuver that brings most matches to a swift end!

Most recently, Sting has added the Scorpion Death Drop to his list. It's a demolishing move used when rivals are already flat on the mat!

Charity work Outside the ring, Sting works tirelessly for charity. He is especially proud of his work with children.

Sting punishes Vampiro with the Scorpion Deathlock.

Dancing defense
When Booker T. is in trouble, he drops to the mat and goes into a breakdancing backspin! Returning to his feet, he strikes back with a flying forearm or a killer kick.

Many talents
Some wrestlers rely on their strength. Others use a high-flying attack. Booker T. is an example of a grappler who can do both!

Booker T.

Booker T. has won seven WCW titles including the WCW World Heavyweight Championship.

His finishing move is called the Ax Kick, and it combines power, speed, and skill. Booker T. swings his muscular leg like an ax, and chops his opponent down to size. Booker T. makes sure that he trains his leg muscles constantly, to keep the Ax Kick effective.

His secondary finishing move, the Missile Drop Kick, is delivered with a flying flip off the top rope.

Owing to the power and skill of these moves, Booker T. has won the WCW TV title six times, more than any other wrestler.

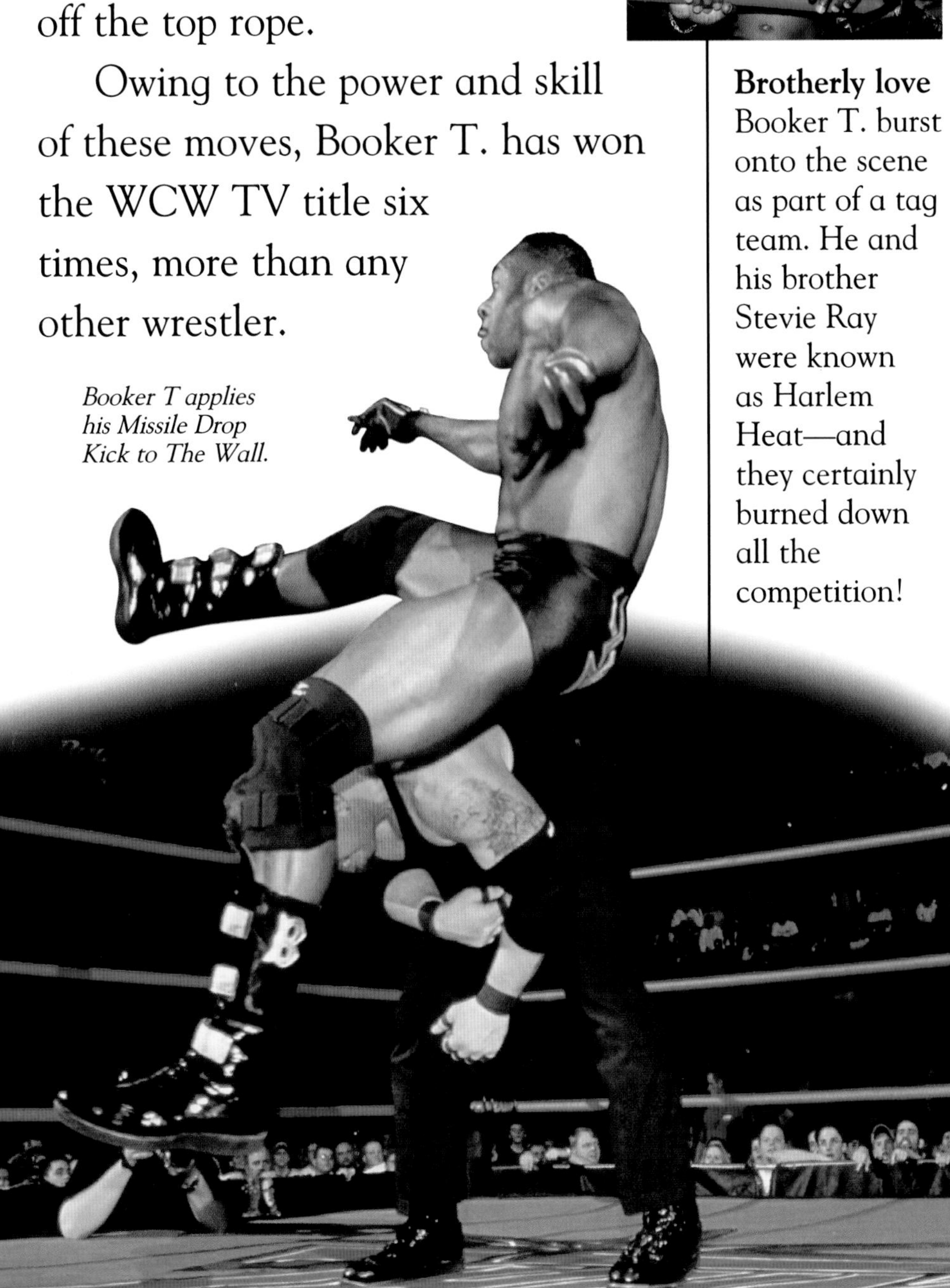

Booker T applies his Missile Drop Kick to The Wall.

Brotherly love
Booker T. burst onto the scene as part of a tag team. He and his brother Stevie Ray were known as Harlem Heat—and they certainly burned down all the competition!

New Blood
Jarrett was the main wrestler in the New Blood. This group was composed of younger wrestlers who were trying to seize control of WCW.

Guitar man
Despite all his talent, Jeff Jarrett constantly breaks the rules. He often carries his guitar into the ring—not to sing his opponent a song, but to use it as an illegal weapon *(right)*.

Jeff Jarrett

Jarrett calls himself "the future of wrestling," and he is one of the most versatile wrestlers in the world. His size—5'10" and 230 pounds—puts him closer to the cruiserweight division, but nonetheless he has won the WCW heavyweight belt three times.

Jarrett's personal finishing move is called the Stroke. To create this, he took a classic wrestling move, called the Russian legsweep, and turned it inside out. The Russian legsweep strikes an opponent in the front of his body, driving him onto his back. But when Jarrett unleashes the Stroke, his poor victim is struck in the back, so the poor wrestler ends up face down on the mat.

Jarrett often uses his strength, his intelligence, and the Stroke to take down much bigger opponents, such as Kevin Nash.

Slap
Nuts
Slap

He skates, too! Before leaving Canada to wrestle in Mexico, Vampiro played hockey and was drafted by the Kingston Ontario Hockey League.

Vampiro

In his ghostly facepaint, Vampiro is a mysterious wrestler.

He is originally from Canada, where he began wrestling, but his career really took off in Mexico. His style, a mix of lucha libre high-flying acrobatics and martial arts, made him a huge hit with Mexican wrestling fans.

Vampiro finally joined WCW in 1999. He fought a series of legendary battles against Kidman, even though he also teamed up with Kidman sometimes!

He also clashed with the wrestler Berlyn in a struggle to dominate WCW. Vampiro said Berlyn's gothic persona was phony.

Dark, moody Vampiro only comes out at night!

Vampiro pretends to check Kidman's pulse!

Vampiro wins his matches with the Nail in the Coffin finishing move. He draws on his upper body strength to lift his opponent, then drives his rival into the mat, before taking a flying leap and landing on his back! Ooof!

Rock 'n' roll!
Vampiro worked as a bodyguard for a pop group before he became a wrestler!

Dr. Franchise
Before joining WCW, The Franchise applied to medical school, hoping to become a doctor.

The Franchise

The Franchise took a standard move, the suplex, and made it his own. His finishing move is called the Pittsburgh Plunge, after his hometown of Pittsburgh.

In the classic suplex, one wrestler grabs his opponent's trunks. But The Franchise catches his victim behind the knee and folds him into a position known as the "small package." Lifting the "package" over his head, The Franchise falls backward to victory. He is very careful as he carries out the move, to avoid seriously hurting his victim.

The Franchise once worked as a teacher, but kept wrestling on the side!

Outsider
The Franchise knows the meaning of the word "outsider." He's left the world of professional wrestling many times, only to return again and again.

During his time with WCW, The Franchise has won a tag team championship with partner Ricky Steamboat. He was also leader of a short-lived group called the Revolution.

Recently, he became a major player in the group New Blood, where he continued his long-running feud with his arch enemy, the legendary wrestler Ric Flair.

It takes every ounce of strength in The Franchise's body to perform the Pittsburgh Plunge.

Kronik

Competing as Kronik, Brian Adams and Bryan Clark won the WCW World Tag Team Championship after only a few months together. These wrestlers may well be the future of tag team wrestling. They are two of the most powerful men in WCW, and their partnership seems unbeatable.

Beginnings
Adams and Clark were originally members of the New Blood. They turned their backs on Eric Bischoff and Vince Russo when they realized that they were just being used, and instead teamed up to form Kronik.

Kronik's finishing move, High Time, is an exercise in math. It starts with the classic body slam. Multiply it by two—that is, two wrestlers executing a double body slam at the same time—and you've got High Time, the low point for any opponent!

It's High Time for a victory as Kronik performs the finishing move.

Strong man
Bryan Clark may well be the strongest wrestler in WCW. Thanks to his incredible conditioning, he can easily lift opponents weighing more than 400 pounds over his head.

Martial arts
Brian Adams studied various martial arts for years, although his wrestling style is anything but "artistic." It's more like search and destroy!

It's not hair! Bam Bam Bigelow has no hair. Instead, his bald head is covered with a tattoo of a giant fireball!

Bam Bam Bigelow

With Bam Bam Bigelow it's all about size and power. His finishing move is called Greetings from Asbury Park, a famous town on the New Jersey shore.

In order to carry out this awesome maneuver, Bam Bam must lift his opponent up over his shoulder. That's where his great strength pays off. The rest of this move is about returning his victim to the mat, and then to the locker room!

After getting his WCW career off to a flying start, Bigelow left the organization and wrestled all over the world. He claimed titles in Japan and Germany, before returning to WCW.

At 6'3" and 369 pounds, Bam Bam Bigelow is a very imposing figure.

Bigelow immediately challenged Goldberg in the middle of the champ's record-setting winning streak. As if that wasn't gutsy enough, Bigelow also challenged Kevin Nash. He offered to wrestle both Nash and Goldberg at the same time! Only a wild man like Bam Bam Bigelow, who has no fear of pain, would relish a match like that.

The Triad
As a member of a tag team called the Triad, Bigelow held the WCW tag team title, along with partners Diamond Dallas Page and Kanyon.

Kanyon receives Greetings from Asbury Park.

Ego clash
Buff was a leader in the New World Order. But when the giant egos of fellow nWo members Hulk Hogan and Scott Steiner became too much for Buff (whose own ego is rather huge, as well), he quit the group.

Buff Bagwell

There has never been a more impressive-looking wrestler than Buff Bagwell. His near-perfect physique is the result of countless hours in the gym. It sets off his movie-star good looks and tremendous athletic ability.

Buff burst onto the scene with a splash in 1990, winning the WCW Rookie of the Year award. He hasn't yet won a championship on his own. However, he has gained four WCW tag team titles, with four different partners, beating such tag team greats as Harlem Heat and the Nasty Boys.

With his winning smile and superb body, Buff's face adorns some of WCW's most popular merchandise.

Buff appeared in the films The Day of the Warrior *and* Return to Savage Beach.

His finishing move is called the Buff Blockbuster. It shows off his conditioning, strength, and agility. Leaping from the second rope, he soars over his opponent, flips forward, and grabs his stunned victim by the back of the head. The poor opponent comes crashing down onto the mat. Game over!

All star
Bagwell is a terrific all-round athlete. He was a baseball player in high school, and later, an amateur boxer. He's also a great golfer and a massage therapist.

Buff performs the Blockbuster on the Cat, during a Road Wild *match.*

Youngster
Rey began wrestling in Mexico at the young age of 16. He actually used to do his homework in the locker room while waiting for his matches to start!

Rey Mysterio, Jr.

Rey Mysterio, Jr. is the undisputed king of the cruiserweights. He has won five WCW cruiserweight titles. His daredevil, no-fear, high-flying aerial maneuvers have brought the Mexican "lucha libre" style of fast-paced athletic wrestling into WCW.

Rey spends almost as much time in the air as he does on the mat. He was named after his uncle, a famous Mexican wrestler.

Rey's high-flying moves expose him to the risk of injury. He has missed several matches due to hurting his knees.

High flying
Back in the 1980s, diving off the top rope was considered too risky. Then Rey burst onto the scene. Now skillful wrestlers often launch themselves from the top rope, adding a new level of excitement to their matches.

Rey flies highest when he unleashes his finishing move, the Huracanrana. When the move begins he is already off the ground, and up on the shoulders of his opponent. With great strength and agility, he executes a backward handspring without letting go of his opponent. That's when the Huracanrana strikes with the force of a hurricane!

Giant killer
Despite being 5'3" and 140 pounds, Rey is not afraid to take on the biggest WCW heavyweights. He's beaten Kevin Nash (all 6'11", 370 pounds of him) and Bam Bam Bigelow (6'3", 369 pounds), earning the nickname "Giant Killer."

Tag team
Kidman has won the WCW cruiserweight championship twice. He has also won two tag team titles, first with Rey Mysterio, Jr., and then with Konnan. Not all of Kidman's partnerships have worked out so well. Once, while he was teamed with Vampiro, the two partners forgot about their opponents and turned on each other!

Kidman

Kidman is one of the few wrestlers to pull off the dangerous maneuver that became his finishing move, the Shooting Star Press.

Even the most experienced wrestlers are too frightened to perform this backward flip off the top rope. But Kidman has great skill and has spent many months training. Now he uses the Shooting Star Press to shoot down some of the biggest names in wrestling.

Kidman has taken his place alongside Rey Mysterio, Jr. as one of the best wrestlers in the cruiserweight division. Perhaps one day he will decide to challenge WCW's heavyweight champions. Who can tell? For now, he's content to tear his way through the cruiserweights, bringing the crowd to its feet with his aerial magic and acrobatics.

Beginnings
Kidman made his debut in WCW in 1996, as part of the group of wrestlers known as "Raven's Flock." He competed under the name "Kid Flash".

Risk
The Shooting Star Press is so risky that even Jushin Liger, who invented the move, won't attempt it any longer.

Cover your face
Some wrestlers, such as Sting (*above*), wear face paint to look more intimidating. Rey Mysterio, Jr. started his career wearing a tradional Mexican wrestling mask for the same reason.

Power and grace

There is no set formula for becoming a successful WCW champion. Some stars use sheer power and physical strength. Others use speed and agility. But there are common threads that bind all professional wrestlers together.

Big Poppa Pump can rely on his bulk to win matches!

Regardless of style—and there are quite a few styles—each wrestler needs commitment, training, and a good battle plan.

It's not enough just to want to be a pro. A young athlete who tries to reach the top of WCW must stay focused on his goal. He must train, day in and day out, conditioning his body, heart, lungs, and mind.

A WCW pro must learn the right way, the safe way, to execute his holds, slams, and maneuvers. Then he and his opponent won't get hurt. He also needs tough mental conditioning to survive both in and out of the ring.

WCW is a world filled with many personalities, egos, and eccentrics. A young wrestler must blaze his own trail, and find a unique look, attitude, and of course, a devastating finishing move.

Then he's on his way to the top!

Glitter and gold
Long-time great Ric Flair is well known for his outrageous costumes. He's achieved golden success in his wardrobe and in the ring!

Mental toughness
It takes tremendous focus and dedication to reach the top. "Heart and mind" are as much a part of the formula as "muscles and moves."

Glossary

Acrobatics
Movements that rely on speed and skill.

Arch enemy
A person's most disliked opponent.

Consecutive
In a row, one after the other without interruption.

Contender
Someone taking part in a competition.

Debut
The first time someone appears somewhere. In this case, the first time someone appears as a WCW wrestler.

Demolished
Destroyed.

Disqualified
Declared the loser because of cheating.

Ego
Part of the mind; your feelings about yourself. People with big egos think very highly of themselves.

Executing
Carrying out, or putting into action.

Executive
A person who is in charge of an organization.

Exploit
To take advantage of someone else

Feud
A long-running quarrel.

Flamboyant
Showy, flashy, loud, drawing attention to oneself.

Intense
Strong, powerful, extreme, severe.

Maintain
To keep up, to keep something going, to continue.

Martial arts
A number of different kinds of self-defense techniques, which began in Asia. Judo and karate are two examples.

Persona
Personality or character.

Pin
In wrestling, to hold an opponent's shoulders to the mat for a count of three. This results in winning the match.

Precision
Exactness, accuracy.

Professional, or "pro"
In sport, someone who earns his or her living through sport.

Psychology
The study of the mind, which tries to explain why people behave the way they do.

Relish
To enjoy or look forward to.

Renegade
Outlaw, outsider, not part of the main group.

Spectacle
A big show.

Status
Rank, position, grade.

Submission hold
A wrestling hold from which an opponent can't escape. It is used to win a match.

Suplex
A move in which one wrestler lifts his opponent into the air, then both wrestlers come crashing to the mat.

Turnbuckles
The padded cushions in each of the four corners of the wrestling ring.

Unleash
To turn loose, to put into action.

Variation
A change, a different way of doing something.